Wales

Poetry for a Nation

Philip John

Front Cover Artwork

by

Paul Humphreys

ISBN: 979-8-3600-3542-8

DEDICATION

For my country, our people, and our future…

CONTENTS

Wales

Wales,
Buried in wild garlic snow,
Somewhere beneath the foliage of an ancient wood,
Where people are wandering in a pitiful blindness,
And sing songs they cannot bring themselves to speak of,
Whilst the beasts in the undergrowth gnaw away
At the flesh of old legends.

The masts of yesterday's martyrs
Are met with a long gone longing,
And centuries of education dictated by conquerors
Leave all bereft of wanting.
Only the terrified, passive peasants left to wither
In the dying bosom of a demoted gentry.

Those sick with forgotten nostalgia are perfect students,
Tomorrow's Welsh doctors for imperial disease,
The terminal illness of a millennia,
How much will be left to choice,
When it comes to being free?

Calling on the doors of terraced valleys,
To wake their ancestors who fought for better days.

Calling on the quiet borders,
To look away from the neighbour's telescope.

Calling on the coastal sleepers,
To rise in defiance and wash the walls of our seas.

Calling on the North resistance,
To rebuild the mountains from the agony of castle ruins.

It is only when the calls come together,
Will an old nation finally stand with the trees once more.
It is only then shall Wales remember herself.

The Princes of Mynydd Dinas

The gallop of invisible horses
Narrated another battle in this silent war.
Two young princes lead the way
Through the decimation of needles and graffiti –
     a cry in the desperate quiet for more generations lost.

With their wooden swords aloft,
They roll through the barren hills of home.
The voice of Y Mab Darogan beckons from the Pen Y Graig,
And in the wind that carries them,
The echoes of an old language sing from scattered chapels.
The shattered eyes of a colliery ruin cast their warning,
To remember the sacrifice of forefathers,
In the mud and the blood – shed for the diamonds of black.

And in the higher plains,
Where warriors fail to fulfil their destiny,
The hopes and dreams are buried
Deep in the green of the valley,
Lost in all our legend.

The first young prince takes a sword too many,
And carried by his compatriot,
Fumbles back down
Through the rocky slopes of this life.
Did he ever leave the battle?
His ghost still wanders the long and winding slivers
Of steep terraced streets
Snaking their way from top to bottom.
Now he is a pirate, dealing in pills and powders,
From the death of opportunity, he is cremated
And whistles wistfully away
In the smoke of the lost industry.

The second young prince rides out into exile
And as the many Rhondda suns are setting,
He travels the land and sea,

In search of all the promises broken by the Empire.
The dragon's tongue still licks the wounds
To taste the flavour of Cymraeg,
But the spirit of Rebecca and the laws of Hywel Dda
Are yet to be reclaimed.

In the visions of Glyndŵr,
The princes must march again today,
Not for blood or gold,
But for social justice,
And the prophecy yet to be fulfilled...
The Princes of Mynydd Dinas are ready to be kings!

Rhiannon

A hole in the void of a twisted sky,
Sucks the light from the land,
And from her hand,
She feeds mankind with wondrous potions,
From an enchanted bag of pure magic,
As she traverses the Island of the Mighty,
Mounted on her horse of silky pearls.

This queen amongst the feudal princes,
This mother of the mystic amongst the accusers,
This goddess amongst dynastic Lords,
This Rhiannon,
A mirage in the majesty of a Celtic dream.

The Women Who Built Wales

A spellcast star aligning Wales with the light of the Moon,
Branwen graced the Brecon sky.
She descended upon the round table,
To summon the great women to their empty seats.

And first she called in soft tones of humble joy, Cranogwen:
"Pioneer of the pen, the Eisteddfod's leading lady,
Join me for a feast of your making."

And then she called for Gwenllian,
"Warrior princess,
A goddess amongst the soldiers of the realm.
In absence of a King, you led the Cymric cause!"

No table would be complete without room for Siwan,
"Lady of Wales, rock of Llywelyn the Great,
Your diplomacy and loyalty to your land and its people,
Spared great bloodshed."

Then Branwen called upon Betty,
"Mrs Campbell,
You are the fire in the belly
Of the Dragonnesses of Tiger Bay –
For black people, for working class people,
You rose above the barriers of social injustice,
A teacher of life in Wales and in the World,
The first and the best."

From Betty, Branwen called upon Betsi…
"Betsi Cadwaladr,
How many souls were saved in your care?
Nurses of prestige tried to hold you back,
But your devotion would not yield,
So I shall cast a spell to raise you from your impoverished end,
To join us at this table for the feast you so well deserve."

Elaine was called beyond the mortal shawl,

"Elaine Morgan,
A champion of your gender,
Projecting your voice from the valleys to the heights
Of science and literature,
Inspiring women to know no bounds!"

Branwen had summoned the women who'd built Wales,
But,
"What of the empty seat?" cried the great women in unison.
"It shall remain empty and reserved forever!" cried Branwen,
"For the last seat is for Mam,
She loved us,
She gave up her voice, her freedom, for us,
And, just like each of you at this table,
She built our Wales for us."

Llywelyn Fychan's Ghost of Steel

As Owain shape shifted through the mystic shadows,
And into the freedom of a Snowdonian night,
A loyal patriot feigned to be a friend of England's Henry,
Led the subjectors through the downs of Deheubarth.

Glyndŵr of Dyfrdwy would rupture the fury of a hell-bent State,
For the folklore of freedom to catch on a millennial wind,
But for the sleeping Cymry to be dreaming instead of dying,
Llywelyn Fychan of Caeo sacrificed the luxuries of the landed gentry,
For torturous annihilation at the hands of all that is evil.

With blueprints built by unknown heroes – hallowed by the gallows,
Cymru breaks bread in a Parliament once more,
And begins again to rewrite the papers of cremated laws.
Llywelyn ap Gruffydd Fychan chose death before treachery,
Where that ghost of steel still guards the castle walls of Llanymddyfri.

In the Suburb of a Dead Town

The lonely streets are quiet tonight,
As the moon gladly tells of the times gone by.
Because he's seen it all,
From the birth of the Queen's rock,
To the warring of the ancient tribes.
But the sleepy houses are tired now,
In the suburb of a dead town.

The rising sun can tell you more,
Of man and boy setting sail for the foreign shore,
To fight in someone else's war.
Of man and boy breaking their backs,
To dig and dig for the diamonds of black.
Mothers, like rocks, holding the fort,
The struggle for freedom waging on.

The place has not lost its voice,
But does not speak of the mystery,
Of this beautiful land,
Steeped in history.
Nothing left to prove,
As I walk atop the rolling green hills,
Staring down,
In the suburb of a dead town.

The Fulling Mill

Before we walked—like hopeless lovers—unto that old fulling mill,
We stopped and, eye to eye,
        saw the world in each other—alive yet still.
Our prayers could not be answered in all our song and dance,
And we knew in that very moment that we'd never get the chance.
A chance to walk again—young and free,
Far beyond the skyline and o'er that greenest lea.
On that day, the simplest of nature's work, so beautiful to me,
The patterns of the shade, cast by shapely leaves,
The (somehow) enchanting song of a single humming bee,
Only echoes of all I saw in you—and oh, how it set me free!

School Boy Friday, Collier Boy Monday

I thought it an adventure,
To give up my sums and follow fy mrawd
Deep down into the wormholes of the Cyfarthfa underworld.
I had to trade my ticket to a better life
For a bit more bara for Mam,
Lamp light in my hand
And lunch box under my arm.

I went down with my butty
And many other men.
They sent me into a coal filled cradle,
Fit more for death than life.
It was there I lost the light in my lamp,
And my little lungs were muffled by the dust,
I wounded my hands and knees,
And though in the darkness I could not see,
I think my blood ran black,
Just like the coal I'd carried on my back.

I called out for my father, my butty, and my brother,
But all that came back was blinding thunder,
And even though the darkness was complete,
The lights went out again,
And that is all I knew of life,
For on Friday I was a school boy,
And on Monday I was a collier boy.

Into the Mystic Mists of Gwent

The glint of the great Silurian shields,
Rise from the ruins of Roman fields.
The ancient Britons take their royal places,
Princes and Kings with ever-changing faces,
And then in they went,
Into the mystic mists of Gwent!

The call of Cynfarch ascends from a church buried deep,
Carried in a cloud above the Dyke so steep.
Here so many Welsh martyrs lie,
Sleeping on the western side of the Wye,
And in they went,
Into the mystic mists of Gwent!

Gruffydd came to stake his claim,
Before the Iron rings and Norman flame.
Chepstow Castle stood in the way,
The gateway to the riches of all who pray,
And in they went,
Into the mystic mists of Gwent!

More medieval prophecies foretold,
Of the Mab Darogan yet to take hold.
Lawgoch was lost before he could win,
A man so mighty betrayed by a sin,
And in he went,
Into the mystic mists of Gwent!

Glyndŵr fought for his people to be free,
A warrior, a scholar, and a father of his country.
Though the demise came at great cost,
Now this old nation would never be lost,
And in he went,
Into the mystic mists of Gwent!

On the beaches of Pembrokeshire he landed,
Henry Tudor came to raise his standard.

Beyond the lands of his forefathers,
Tragedy struck his firstborn Arthur,
And in he went,
Into the mystic mists of Gwent!

The landscape changed by a turbulent past,
But Wales was a legacy promising to last,
Universities, institutions, and a Parliament leading the way,
Glyndŵr's great vision is coming into play,
So many centuries after he went,
Into the mystic mists of Gwent!

Still there is poverty plaguing the lands,
More work to be done to bring justice in these hands,
To forge a new vision and future for the young,
Heroes in waiting and new songs to be sung,
But never forget those who went,
Into the mystic mists of Gwent!

The Black Rivers of 1905

Too little.
And too much
Of faith,
In visions beyond the burning face.
In all the years of hungry struggle,
In smothering pits, rising to dark
From the dark.
What were the birds singing on the 10th March?

The rivers ran black and the green was buried
With the men, and boys, who never came back.
And now to walk with ghosts in Clydach Vale,
We must break the silence to tell them,
Those prisoners of their own time,
That their souls fell into the black rivers
To run so clear again.

When, that eve, the explosion
Reaped the earth of its salt,
And took the lives of the voiceless,
The sun had set on the black hills
Leaving orphans, widows, families,
To grieve in life
 —unto death.

So if you're ever passing
The shrine that sleeps by the lake,
Remember to tell them,
That shift was all for us.
A better life, built by hands and pure hearts,
It is they who turned these black rivers to glân.

National Health

When your life is shaped organically,
From a ground of worker's seeds,
And when those same workers pick your fruit,
Or pick your black diamonds from the coal face,
To fuel the everlasting fire in your belly,
You've a birthplace, a breeding ground,
For a vision of social justice,
Burning through the barriers of this unnatural order.

In the Eastern vales of song,
There was such a seed,
One with less light, less water, less room,
But evermore heart than all the privileged gardens in bloom.
Beyond the summers of the formative years,
We were graced with a gift from a cup of humanity.
A service to be fought for, tooth and nail,
And whilst there are those who are willing to fight,
The national health shall refuse to fail.
And tell them to put their cheques aside,
Never a matter for the illusionary numbers,
But the flowers of humanity,
Blooming from those impoverished seeds,
And the labour of love,
Embraced by the people, from Bevan, above.

The Three Feathers of Mametz Wood

Three wrote letters home, from hell,
In dark waves between shot and shell,
Amongst the senseless void beyond summer's death,
So many lungs of the 38th battalion would take their final breath.

Two letters made it home to tell,
That a missing letter would go unread,
It died aside a large Welsh heart,
Brave as the war cry of a Mametz lark.

As morning called the world to arms,
Soldier watching soldier – bayonets at the charge,
Desperate eyes stare deep into dying eyes,
And they'd both hear the devil's cries.

A fatherless child, in the hope of the homefront, still waits
For a name to be etched in memorial slate,
And those who came back from the slaughter,
From their miles of mud to mother and to daughter,
Had a lifetime of carrying restlessly heavy ghosts from the wood,
Before their time came to go back to a place where no man should.

Now they are the fabric of space, and time, and everything,
To have given themselves, completely, and asked in return for nothing,
There's a place in the wood where three ostrich feathers float through every tree,
And though they cannot cleanse unspeakable ills,
Let them be endless, weightless,
For it is they who set us free.

Rebellion

It has been said,
Spoken by eyes above ivory towers,
That we're sleeping in sadness
Beyond the fortified fear of another rebellion.
Well, let's say this, then,
That we'll tell you of rebellion…

Rhodri the Great,
In our Chronicle of the Princes,
Expelled the might of Vikings,
And laid down his life in the fight to
Hold those Saxons back.

From the gracious chair of the bards,
Our Lord Rhys of Deheubarth,
Is still singing of his own immortality,
As he banished the Norman brutes from the
Aberteifi,
And built the stones of Wales with a victory
Sealed in Eisteddfod.

Llywelyn the Last was far from our last,
And Madog rose from the rubble of the resistance,
To keep an ancient flame burning,
But as his light went out in captive darkness,
Soon came Llywelyn Bren
To carry the torch of freedom's cry.
He met his end in bloody quarters,
But those who lived by their sword,
Would feel the wrath of a dragon's vengeance,
Dispensing of evil Despensers.

Who but Glyndŵr would never be a prize for wanton oppressors,
And instead would live forever as the foundation
Of a country built to last.
Though the centuries faded into the repressed of sickly woe,
That old phantom fluttered in the bellies of the industrial slaves,

As Dic Penderyn and the miners of the Merthyr rising
Battled against the shackles of the insatiable monsters of coal,
And a gross miscarriage of justice
Saw a man of Merthyr a martyr.

It begs another big question,
When more miners were to fight,
Shoulder to shoulder,
With Republicans across the waves,
They gave their lives in a fight against the fascists,
Yet at home,
The peasantry still left to rot,
And pay rent,
Rent for homes that should be their own,
How can we let it be so?

The bloodied swords of yesterday's sacrifice
Will sit behind the glass,
And pen and voice, and bricks and toil,
Will be tomorrow's fight.
The flame has not gone out,
My longing old friend,
The call is coming again…
You know…
… and so…
… when it calls…
Don't forget to answer!

The Day They Filled the Chapel

"I want this chapel filled…" he said,
And, oh, it was filled,
With the emptiness of unfathomed agony,
A godless morgue,
That no mother should have to bear witness.

It always seemed as though time would wait for no man,
But still it waits in Aberfan,
Somewhere in the rubble and sludge of a negligent evil
The one that descended like deathly earth,
Onto tomorrow's salt of the earth.

Springs of death coughed up the neglect of corporate men,
And stole a sacred gift, not just from 144 of them,
But the future of those who were left,
In the burning flames of eternal trauma.

"Don't touch my room, Mam, I'll finish playing later…"
Just like any other day,
Except for when the school clock stopped ticking,
And the toys never got to finish their story,
And there's a light in Mam's eye
That went out forever.

Dwynwen

The characters in our childhood theatres
Tell our fireside stories of love and heartache.
Of logs burning to the sound of harps,
Of folk songs in the enchantment of ancient saints.
And if those old tales are long to tell,
Let them be told well into nightfall,
And burst into a life of midnight dreams.

In dreams she'll be there to sing sweetly of a wholesome love,
She'll be there to cry into the haunting waves of Ynys Llanddwyn
Healing the deep, centenarian wounds of ours,
Yet with the pain of Brychan's promise to another man,
Dwynwen's heart would never heal,
A burning hiraeth,
A yearning, gaping ache for her Maelon, never to be,
But still, she stands in the archway of romance,
Shining on the dancing lovers of freedom.

A Robin in the Eagle's Nest

A Robin in the Eagle's nest,
Dwells on the edge of old,
Where the watery blood of two rivers converge,
The Severn bridges join across the threshold.

The Brythonic vein of the Wye,
Carries the weight of all who came west,
But there shall be no country for the young,
If the lifeblood is poisoned by human conquest.

The Robin left with a call for Spring,
Carried by a lyrical wind from a quiet slope,
Two rivers meet their open mouth,
Don't bite the hand that feeds it with hope.

The School of Life

Framed in blue with proud golden boundaries,
Our kingdom and our playground.
Bricks as old as time, and the corridors made for little people,
And the walls filled with wonder, to nurture and nourish the saplings,
Binding our roots so strongly.
What a fine morning it must be, to hear a hundred little voices,
Singing for a Calon Lân with all the joy of youth,
Or to see a summer fair, blooming like the Garden of Eden on a grand
opening to one and all.

Though to you tall walkers, grown up to see beyond our walls,
It looks as though our sanctuary is oh, so very small,
But, you see, we paint our pictures in whirlwinds of the imagination,
Inside this is our universe, and in that, all the worlds we made.
Worlds where no other would laugh at any of our wildest dreams,
But keep us believing in all there is to achieve.

As all the little voices deserted every classroom,
The cast iron gates resigned themselves to rust.
Holy building, you stood for several hundred years,
As long as the wise old oaks that stood guard between our valley.
But as the colours crumbled,
They came to take your soul.
Crashing through your walls, I hear so many songs,
And ghosts that sing through emptiness to fill the night with tales of
warmer times.
No trace that you were ever there,
But for those of us that now remain,
We thank you for being our happiest time,
Embarking all of us on this ride, with a one way ticket to life.

An Unconquerable Tongue

Red wings that carried them,
Far along a solitary shore,
Where the Princes of Gwynedd had gathered before.
The bittersweet lifeblood,
And an unconquerable tongue,
The real treasure.

Magicians in the mountains,
Under the spell of a colonial craze,
Carrying the cost through a hellish, bloody maze.

Eternal rebellion,
Transcending the myth and forefathers' legend.
The last man standing shall not shake the hand,
Nor break his oath to his father's land.
His final, unhindered swindle,
Relentless and unforgiving,
Lay it to rest but forget me not.

Only we could remember,
The bloodshed and selfless sacrifice,
As we were beaten out of words,
Given unto us by the brave warriors,
Who would not fall in the face of defeat.
Carry we did,
A language of unquestionable immortality,
Through all adversity,
And into the light.

Running Through the Cynon

The stones of the ordinary,
They lived and breathed,
And died to be unturned.
Today, we unturn.

And who should escape,
Faster than the speed of legend,
Guto Nyth Brân
Running through the Cynon.
You couldn't catch his heart,
For his spirit would haunt you ever after.
The world would stay forever on his heels,
Only catching whispers of that shooting star,
From the gateway to the Rhondda,
Who set the mountains alight
All across our valleys,
To face his greatest calling,
Against the Prince of Bedwas.

Under the watchful eye of Siân o'r Siop
He had conquered athletes far and wide,
From other local challengers,
To the best in all of Britain's isles.
Guto's heart retired in the arms of Siân,
And the bosom of his home,
But then that Prince came calling,
For one more race to be run.

Out ahead went the Prince of Bedwas,
Marching on to take the sprinter's mantle,
Lay his flag as the bearer of tomorrow's race.
But as the hills came rolling down,
The runners clambered up.
Warriors new and old,
Stars with new orbits,
And old horses going out with one more
Jolt of lightening love,

For Guto would climb the hill a champion once more,
Collapsed in the arms of his Siân,
Never to rise again.

Now the Ras Nos Galan is run again each year,
But you best keep up your pace,
For the ghost of Guto
Shall never give up on his race!

Borderlands

The cloud edge, still ablaze
From the far reaching flames of the setting sun,
Is doused in the silken showers of moonrise,
And in this ancient field, the sheep deserted,
I could stand for all the hours left in light,
Before the stillness, the blackness,
Banishes all that today will ever be.

'Twas as if the sun had fallen,
In flurries of miniature lionesses,
But it could not have fallen,
For still it floated above, warming our Earth,
More than ever before.

'Twas as if the sky had fallen,
A twirling token of wild blue yonder,
A butterfly enchanting the eyes of the lost.
But the heavens were still intact,
So perhaps it was just a token from Spring,
With a promise that tomorrow
Shall be brighter than today.

'Twas as if I had fallen,
'Neath the cherry blossom at Monk's Rest,
Not a sound
But for the rushing of the old brook,
Today is just.

In Gwenllian's Dreams

I hope he came to you in your dreams, Princess,
I hope he came to you in your dreams.
In your shackled hours of shrouded sanctity,
Deprived of all you were,
In tongue and from destiny.
I hope he came to see you,
In full form and speaking to you
In a language you were born to know.
I hope he told you of the sacrificial freedom,
And showed you of your land, your people,
And where your soul belongs.

If he came to you, you'll know,
You're another of our warriors of bardic flame,
Inside a conquered shell,
Bearing your ennobled name.

I hope when you departed,
You went to him to hear it for yourself,
That your legend is safe
In the annals of Hen Gymraeg.

Now the crumbling castles of King Edward,
Are crowned with Y Ddraig Goch,
And history will sign your name
Just as it was always meant to be,
Gwenllian, Princess of Wales.

The Welsh Atlantis

The Welsh Atlantis breathes beneath Llyn Celyn,
Where the people vote en masse,
In a village of native speaking,
With a knowing sense of all of our nation's past.

The Blue Books have no place in the library of Capel Celyn,
And they've sent them out amidst the flow of the Afon Treweryn,
For no more shall the telescope be leering from outside in,
No more shall they suffer from the evils of imperial sin.

When will the same be said for the surface dwellers above the flooded plains?
When will the telescope be turned completely on its head?
When will the people salvage the sheer will?
When will they stop waiting for answers anywhere but within?
When?

Celtic Stone

I wish I could talk to the Nevern cross,
And see all as it was, in the eyes of the oldest Celt.
If you hung the treacherous wood of the Welsh Not
Around its neck,
The sign would rot from inside out and the remains would scatter like
An escaping bile of sawdust,
But the Celtic stone would stand in an ancient defiance,
Rooted like the trees born long before its neighbour - a house of God,
And long before its followers,
The graves of nameless sacrifice.
Did you show Saint Brychan the way?
Did you see the mighty Arthur on a lonesome day?
Did you warn the conquerors of the wrath of a Welsh winter?
Did you sleep through centuries of prayer?
And, most importantly of all,
What is it that you see now?

Organic

The fabric of my faculties,
Threadbare as the worn out carpet,
To an old coal fire,
Burning through the night.

I washed away the toil,
In a rustic and rusted tin,
Somewhere in that simplicity,
I was whole, free from sin.

My Country is in My Bones

I remember feeling my country,
In my unshaped growing bones,
Mesmerised by fantastical folklore,
Eyes always open,
Heart yearning.

… but then the Suits from elsewhere,
Came with their hammer and chisel,
To chip away the Welsh from our bones,
And leave us as Children of the Empire,
Aspiring to the exceptionalism of foreign rule,
With a mocking disinterest in who we really are,
Beginning a false, indoctrinated nonsense such as this…

"Their language is backward and useless, be done with it,"
"Teach them about our Royalty until they've no whisper of their own,"
"We'll fill their bellies with the pride of victory, so that they are
indifferent to their emptiness on the Union Jack and the Royal Crests."
"Ignore their voices in our parliament, veto their laws, extract their
wealth and return them with nothing, because they matter not"

And, after all that vile exploitation, still I have come full circle.
No matter the mould, or the force-fed garbage of an overprivileged
crew from the sour leftovers of an Eton mess,
Those chipped Welsh bones healed in a fusion of defiance…
"Our beautiful language survived and thrives"
"Our past could not be burned, for the flames are eternally
extinguished by immortal ghosts."
"We'll legislate our way back from the slumber of old law"
"Listen to our voices, listen to our hearts. We are still here."

The Heart of the Valley

The heart of the valley is beating below,
Hidden in the hills where clear rivers flow,
The blackest of pits from days gone by,
Voices of men who are lost in time.

The heart of the valley is beating below,
Where choirs of children filled chapels with song,
Forests of freedom,
A place you belong.

The heart of the valley is beating below,
Row upon row of boxes fill the void.
Humble and hungry,
What is that noise?
The beat goes on,
But for how long?

People of passion and spirit remain,
The heart of the valley is not beating in vain,
The fire still burns in the mountains,
The dragon is waiting within.

Where the Heart Is

A walk out in the world again,
All it takes,
The smell of home in the street,
And it's not so different anymore.

The lost and the found,
And I know now,
However upside down it gets,
After life's trauma,
And out of the clutches of chaos,
I can go back to this place.
I am this place.
My rock, my heart.

Christmas in the Rhondda

I've shaken the bug from the roots of my travelling soul,
And on my worn out gypsy shoes the road has taken its toll.
Yet lights shall still mark the hillside at the dead of night,
And I know for as long as they carry my flame in their eyes so bright,
I'll be home for another Christmas in the Rhondda tonight.

Delinquent stars carried me from high above the Rhigos,
Now my clapped-out wings will settle with only this valley to cross.
The wind is singing of home as it whispers through the chill,
I walk on down the terraced rows and beside the window sills,
And my mountains roll like dominoes to Treherbert's highest hills.

Not a ghost is stirring but for snow-soft footsteps crunching down,
'Ar gau' the sign hung in the windows of Treorchy's colourful town,
Far from dead –they are sleeping–oh, how I long for my own bed.
Pitter-patter on past Pentre and I shake my sleepy head,
No pint of ale in Llwynypia but onwards I must go instead.

The Tonypandy moonrise is singing the carols of my childhood,
As it spins a web of shimmering silk where the old colliery stood.
And now my legs feel as heavy as that legend Tommy Farr,
When he'd fought his final fight–had I really come this far?
I look straight up above me to try to find his star.

I walked upon the footsteps of the miners of 1910,
A fight for social justice for ordinary working men.
I passed by the shop once owned by Willie Llewellyn,
Who played against the All Blacks in a famous rugby win,
Folklore says that's why the miners never smashed his windows in.

I hope that when the Rhondda sun should rise tomorrow,
The lakes of Clydach Vale will wash away my sorrow,
And that I've time enough to visit the miners' shrine,
To those who gave all they had, let them rest in peaceful rhyme,
Now the swans take sail in hope of a better time.

Not long now before I see all of those old faces,

Only the people of the valley know how much we love these places.
I head for Penygraig–top of the rock–in these higher plains of home,
A sea of lost memories washes over me as I'm standing here alone,
I know I will always return from wherever I may roam.

The golden lights of Williamstown trim my street with song,
As I stumble up those crooked steps–oh so very long,
There are many places I have had to wander,
But now I hear choirs sing to me from over yonder,
Yes, tonight I am home for another Christmas in the Rhondda.

The Settlement

The storms of the epic voyage of 1865,
Promised of the promised land,
And Porth Madryn was born.
A place of home, a thousand miles from home,
Where Cymraeg, and song and dance,
Might escape from conquered, perished lands,
And prosper in this new world - Y Wladfa.

They came without the tyranny,
For they knew too much of that at home,
And they sailed a ship from Lerpwl,
All aboard the Mimosa, 153 of the Cymri.

Sold a false promise of heaven, arriving in a desert hell,
Battered and flushed into despair by the brutal floods,
A terrifying, scorched plain in need of great sacrifice,
Of toil, starvation, and broken backs,
To tame the flames of the Patagonian wilderness,
And cultivate a world they may never see.

The perseverance of a people,
And the building of tribal bridges,
Brought a newfound civilisation,
With windmills, chapels, and that old tongue,
Trelew and Trevelyn the ancestral legacy -
Gwlad Newydd y Cymry.

Breaking the Cycle

Born a neighbour to these wretched estates,
Where friends caved in to a drugged up fate,
Thinkers cannot thrive in the stench of rusty needles
      and burnt-out leaves.
Intellect was a disease.

If you find yourself so far behind before it's even begun,
You start to wish yourself a way of closing the mind to potential,
So you join the party of the existential.
I don't care why we are really here,
I just want to feel my way through the dark.

You know there's a raffle going but it's not what you were sold,
Education the ticket for a ride, for the ones so bold.
I suppose it's a blessing to some kind of comfort,
So you can worry about the ozone instead of the dole,
But you still find yourself in a maze of mediocrity,
Pulling at the strings of the suburban dreamers
      and their flexible friends,
You've climbed every level–greed and hypocrisy doesn't seem to end.

A poetic license doesn't promise you anything that's worth its salt,
But maybe this voice, if only for a second, will get the world to stop.
Let's take it back to the start, right to the very heart,
Show them that there's hope even if there's nothing left,
Maybe we can break the cycle–a platform for those who are next.

Borders of the Soul

The crackling timber shot a licking orange flame,
Climbing up the chimney, far from the reach of the ashen wastelands.
We held our thoughts together as the night began to fall,
Waiting long and hard–would the summer arrive at all?

Alas! The cinders of this longest evening are banished by the sun,
And to us, in love, the harpless songs of the sky are all that's left of
February's rain.
Birds fly o'er these mythical borders, and the fragments we left at either
side,
Connect us here in unison,
        and spare us of the pain.

Though we know the time is short and soon our days slip into modest
hours,
Still we sit here in cottage gardens, consumed by ancient flowers.
Let us not depart or become estranged from the pieces of each other
that we carry inside,
Let us lay our hats at the border,
        and soothe our restless hearts and minds.

King Arthur's Mountains

The ivory wind-cloud's breath takes yours away,
And changes the flight of a raven lost in a world of shrikes.
Whilst in the quiet confidence of King Arthur's mountains,
The light bursts through and shape shifts along the cliffs - a renegade
hunting the poltergeists of Brycheiniog.

The deep moods of the weather are locked in a duel with the swooping
of the slopes,
And the summer could just as well be winter,
A warning from the heavens sent many times before,
The spells of myths and legends,
At work on the top of the world.

Steady as the walk through the windows of the past,
The billowing blast of Welsh wind stops mid-flight,
And in that void of silent hymns,
They will live again as tomorrow's kings.

Our Voice

Manors, mansions, castles,
Luxurious architecture built
      by the extravagant speculators of the gentrified highflyers,
All celebrated, preserved, maintained,
      and showcased as the story of the ruling class,
Told by the victors,
And sold to the rest.

Age old chapels, ghostly ruins of remote terraced rows
      of the barracks of Snowdonia's quarrymen,
The coal miners' institutions,
      quaint stone schools that taught us through our troubles,
      small and proud theatres,
      working men's and social clubs,
Left to rot and crumble,
Or replaced by developers
      with soulless stacks of misplaced profit blocks,
What about our voice?
What about our journey and our past?
For we were here too,
And tomorrow should know about it.

The Little Things

The holy waters of St David,
In their evocation of an implacable song,
Erupts in the earliest summers of our years,
And the voices,
Once scarce in a sanctuary of unburdened silence,
Are rising like the field of a thousand leeks.

Hark Aberteifi!
The tornados of autumn's golden rain,
Are sure to enrich these earnest pilgrims,
To guide them through all the winter,
Long as it may be,
And the world to be
Would do well to take heed,
Of the monastic simplicity of this self-denying shepherd.

When the dawn of spring's saviour glows,
If but nothing is taken in thought or reflection,
Let it be remembered, on 1st March,
As well as each and every day…
Do the little things.

Back in the Hood

I long for the dregs
The dirt and the bloodshed,
Scoundrels rolling through the mud,
I shudder and shiver in my own blood.

I long to be back on the slabs,
Back in the hood, the boys and their tags.
I should've stayed behind,
And sometimes I wonder who made up my mind.

I long to show Mr A that he doesn't have to blow it,
His kid doesn't know it,
Prison for a stopgap but not much to clean,
Permanent filth returning to the street.

I long to know for sure,
If they'd have dragged me down to their sewer.
If I'd stuck around with Mr A and the crew that stalk the street,
Purposeless souls, like islands without feet,
No sight of the continent of opportunity and hope,
Just old Mr B and his big bag of dope.

I long to clean Mr C, blight on blind youth,
Not much of a start but not an excuse,
I wonder if he votes in the name of Llywelyn,
Doesn't even know him nor how to spell it.

I long to walk the wastelands and the children's battlefields,
Where I lost a lot of good friends and almost myself.
But I had a rock, a family, and a shield.

I long to see what I might have seen,
Not that longing should wipe the slate clean,
I'll still be here on the threshold, where I've always really been.

The Welsh Are Not the Dead Relatives of Your Dreams

The Welsh are not the dead relatives of your dreams,
The weather worn faces flashing in the flickering of a miner's lamp,
Deep beneath the chasms of the confidence of consciousness,
In a coal-less, native prince-less, irretrievable passage of bygones.
No. The Welsh are living. The Welsh are alive.

The Welsh are not crawling around in a Western attic,
Waiting for the rapture and all their hallows to be hollowed,
For their own words to be so distant that they are no longer their own,
In a cold and heartless wasteland to be laid to rest.
No. The Welsh are radical. The Welsh are changing.

The Welsh are not settling for meagre slices of self-determination,
Tossed a salmon, and breadcrumbs, with the deficit on the bill,
To be expected to be happy as the anonymous 'et cetera',
The limping veteran in sight of the fountain of youth.
No. The Welsh are here. The Welsh are ready.

Victory

The furnace of fear burns deep within,
Walking through the pantheon,
Judged by all that walked before,
But glory was not made in that moment,
It was built by the battered hands and etched from the rugged stone.

When the fortress is ready to hold the dragon before the flight,
When the mighty have fallen and death has abided the heroes,
You will walk free from the forest,
Free from the gateway of the guardians,
Where it will be found.
Not framed in gold nor held upon the top of the world,
But standing and staring at all that is left,
When victory is yours.

Delicate Hours

Beyond the boughs that bind our hearts,
From springs, the God of all life, streams ebb and flow
       down through our vale.
Watch the lamb as it learns to run, to laugh, and to sing,
You just might learn it too, before the end of spring.

The grey of winter, howling out its final moon,
Makes a morning's safe passage for the hare
       to meet a garrison of flowers yet to bloom,
But, this, not a promise life will never pass you by,
For it is a precious world of oh, so very delicate hours.

Before the world lives and breathes another spring,
Count your friends—not the ones bought
       on an enchanting summer's eve,
But the ones who walked with you
       when the day drifted into a harsh winter's night.
And with those friends, lose your worldly possessions,
Not the honeysuckle or Mother's milk,
But all the silver, gold and Devil's dust.
Because in the garden of a precious world in oh, so very delicate hours,
You are rich enough.

Morgannwg's Spirit

I saw a butterfly-rise,
Bewitching all Morgannwg,
From the hills to the north of Cardiff,
It was Iestyn,
Last true Prince of Glamorgan.
And as his wings tilted downwards,
He was joined by two other butterflies,
And floating there amidst the blood red sky,
Their wings spelled out the chevronels,
Borne on the coat of arms.

And though the lands of the southern Cymri,
Were stolen long ago,
It was the working people,
Ground into ground,
Who kept the spirit of a nation alive,
Through words, through art and legend,
Mining out the minerals of Mother Earth.

Sacrifice can cut so deeply,
Suffering can burn so slowly,
Sorrow can scorch so discreetly,
But sanctity can sing for the timelessness of existence.

Innocence

Untouched by the weight of a heavy world,
Before the first, fatal kiss,
In the grand old garden, the closest to bliss.
Stood in a street so familiar,
The only one that may have ever been.
I was lost picking berries,
Then falling through the ferns,
In a forever place.

Faces I know, I love,
They turn with the ticking of the hand.
Holy houses fall through the seasons,
And I lament.
I lament for all that was promised is lost,
Though it stayed for long enough,
Until friends had flown,
And wise old mentors had resigned.

And as the world around decays,
So do people, and time itself.
But slow enough to savour,
Every ember of youth.

An Ode to Llywelyn

Dear Prince,

I saw the 21st century marked by the shade of a timeless granite obelisk – it asked the sun to break the clouds we've carried since you died here in Cilmeri. I stepped down to the well, feeling sickened by the terminal weight of broken shards of time. Something in the way the crows fly here, tells me that the world did end. The universe stopped. But if the universe is eternity, then so are we, the ones at one with the breeze still blowing dead leaves – they'll feed the soil that keeps these trees alive.

Your grandfather, the great, watches over Conwy now, and waits, and waits. Oh, blessed time, how long has it been now – a thousand years? I sometimes wonder if it has always felt that way. And your children's children would fight in tragic wars, shedding the gift of lifeblood for a freedom to be dormant in the mountains, the rivers, and the valleys far and wide. Better that than a freedom lost, a freedom dead.

So, for all your strategy, for all your diplomacy, and, without trepidation, your sacrifice, you stand shoulder to shoulder with the patriots, on which we now stand to keep our heads above the water. For when the sun sets and shrouds your shrine in the darkness of a bodiless grave, it'll rise again, time after time. An ode then, to you, Llewelyn, but also to the nameless, and the voiceless, without whom there would be no land for which the sun could rise from beneath. But thank you, for being the princely root of dignity. For all that we were, all that we are, and, most importantly, all that we can be!

Sleep well,

Yours truly,

Cymru.

Valley Ghosts

To shrink in the apparitions of December haze,
Like magic,
Whilst reflecting on the frozen sound,
Trapped in the universe of a childhood bedroom,
Is a cause to cheer triumphantly with the slide
Of the sinewy reels of an old tape cassette.

Take me in.
Take me through a portal of a dimension
Of the turning of a new millennium.
In the valleys we were raised by ghosts,
And now we, ourselves, are ghosts.

To look around in the cultural rubble,
So tragic,
Whilst floating above the old ground,
Trapped in a microcosm of unknowing,
Is a cause to cry uninhibitedly with the drift
Of the smoky dreams of valley ghosts.

Reincarnation

Rolling, tumbling at the water's edge,
Black lambs suckling on the whitest sheep,
The gatherer of daffodils sheds tears for the travellers,
As the intrepid move on and the world goes by.

Standing atop the mountains,
Where the weeds move upward,
And the rocks crumble into dust,
Blown by the wind toward the beaten track,
A rusted red gate promises the wanderers of the adventures of the past.

Sanctuary found in the fountains of the forgotten,
The quiet chords of birdsong floating in the air,
And just for a fleeting moment,
You were never really there.

Song of Hiraeth

The sea has sung to the sky,
As I stand on the shoulders of patriots,
With a heart singing of the great saints.

The sea has sung my language,
As I stand on a mountain,
With a heart singing of hiraeth.

The Red Rivers (of Owain Glyndŵr)

The lions were passive in the Principality,
As second-class subjects to colonial invaders,
Rich in heritage but impoverished by penal laws
          and thankless Lords,
Pillaged peasants held to ransom in the iron ring,
Extended to the Uchelwyr with hands tied behind backs.
Until Henry the usurper wronged the wrong man,
And out of the Uchelwyr rose the learned linguist
          and masterful warrior,
To champion the cause of the voiceless.

Crowned true Prince at Machynlleth,
And at Harlech he drew the map of a future Wales,
Owain Glyndŵr with his masterplan –
A foundation of education in the spirit of aspiration,
Never without great cost to himself and his nation.

As the chieftain of guerrilla warfare ruptured through the State,
The dragon spilled blood and red rivers
          pumped through the mountains and the vales,
The battle of Bryn Glas a deathly birthplace of alliance
          and forsaken Earls,
Glyndŵr, heart of Wales, a legend of defiance in the face of evil.
In ecclesiastical devastation and a land of desolation,
Foreign politics ebbed on the fine lines of the Cymric shores.
Henry of Monmouth would inherit a bankrupt throne,
After endless resource to subdue the conflated Welsh cause,
The famished and the dead, could hold out no more.

The cantrefs demolished and the teulu in tatters,
Still he would not be forsaken,
Still he would not be found.
Just as the storms answered to his command,
The mists of the mountains enshrined his devotion.
In the mythical winds of Wales,
He did not die…

From lions passive to lions rampant,
As the dragon stirs from the deep,
Bardic whispers of tomorrow's justice
Shall wake the Cymru from its ancient sleep.

ABOUT THE AUTHOR

Philip John is a Welsh poet and writer from the Rhondda Valleys, graduating from the University of South Wales in 2014 before working and living across the border in Bristol. He has since returned to Wales and now resides in Monmouthshire. Philip has previously had three volumes of poetry published – Home Truths (2018), Searching for Seahorses (2020), and Songs of Youth (2021). Drawing from his experiences of working-class Wales and beyond, his work explores the human condition, nature, history, the environment, and the existential questions in the search for purpose. He was announced as a finalist in the Page Turner Writing Award 2022 and has performed poetry readings at arts festivals, on BBC Radio, and as part of musical collaborations.

Printed in Great Britain
by Amazon